PIANO · VOCAL · GUITAR

# THE BEST JAZZ STANDARDS EVER

ISBN 978-0-7935-2958-2

**HAL•LEONARD®**
CORPORATION

7777 W. BLUEMOUND RD. P.O. BOX 13819 MILWAUKEE, WI 53213

Visit Hal Leonard Online at
**www.halleonard.com**

# THE BEST JAZZ STANDARDS EVER

# ALL OF ME

Words and Music by SEYMOUR SIMONS
and GERALD MARKS

You took my kiss-es and you took my love,___ You taught me how to

care; Am I to be___ just the rem-nant of___ a

# ALL THE THINGS YOU ARE

## from VERY WARM FOR MAY

Lyrics by OSCAR HAMMERSTEIN II
Music by JEROME KERN

Time and a-gain I've longed for ad-ven-ture, some-thing to make my heart beat the fast-er. What did I long for? I nev-er real-ly knew. Find-ing your love I've found my ad-ven-ture,

# APRIL IN PARIS

Words by E.Y. HARBURG
Music by VERNON DUKE

# AUTUMN IN NEW YORK

Words and Music by
VERNON DUKE

17

# THE BLUE ROOM

## from THE GIRL FRIEND

Words by LORENZ HART
Music by RICHARD RODGERS

# BEWITCHED
## from PAL JOEY

Words by LORENZ HART
Music by RICHARD RODGERS

He's a fool and don't I know it, But a fool can have his charms;

I'm in love and don't I show it, Like a babe in arms.

Love's the same old sad sen - sa - tion, Late - ly I've not slept a wink,

# BEYOND THE SEA

Words and Music by CHARLES TRENET,
ALBERT LASRY and JACK LAWRENCE

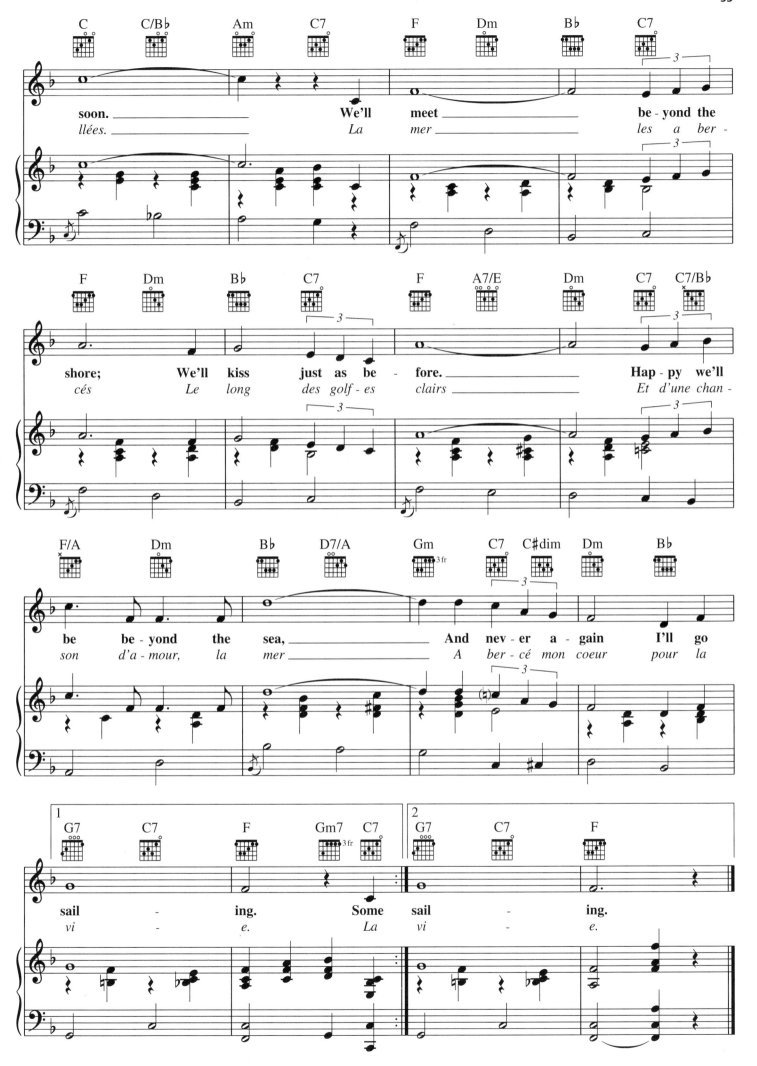

# BLAME IT ON MY YOUTH

Words by EDWARD HEYMAN
Music by OSCAR LEVANT

# BLUESETTE

Words by NORMAN GIMBEL
Music by JEAN THIELEMANS

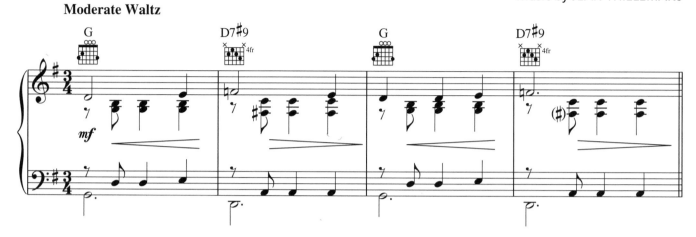

Poor lit-tle, sad lit-tle blue Blues-ette.
Long as there's love in your blue heart Blues to ette share,

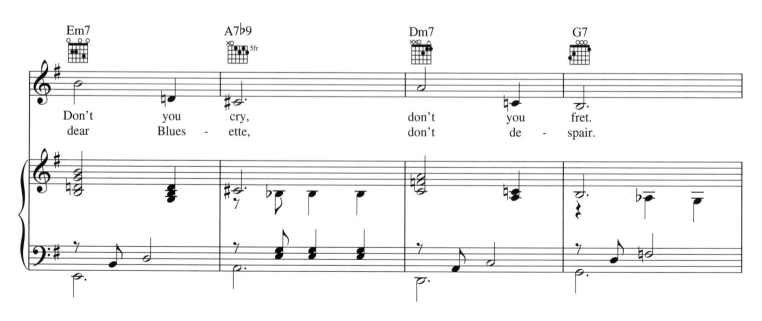

Don't you cry, don't you fret.
dear Blues-ette, don't de - spair.

# BODY AND SOUL

Words by EDWARD HEYMAN,
ROBERT SOUR and FRANK EYTON
Music by JOHN GREEN

48

# BUT BEAUTIFUL

Words by JOHNNY BURKE
Music by JIMMY VAN HEUSEN

Love is fun-ny or it's sad, or it's quiet or it's mad; It's a good thing or it's bad, but beau-ti-ful!

# CALL ME IRRESPONSIBLE

## from the Paramount Picture PAPA'S DELICATE CONDITION

Words by SAMMY CAHN
Music by JAMES VAN HEUSEN

# CAN'T HELP LOVIN' DAT MAN

## from SHOW BOAT

Lyrics by OSCAR HAMMERSTEIN II
Music by JEROME KERN

Fish got to swim ___ and birds got to fly, ___
Tell me he's la - zy, tell me he's slow, ___

I got to love ___ one man till I die. ___
Tell me I'm cra - zy, may - be I know. ___

Can't help lov - in' dat man ___ of

# CARAVAN
## from SOPHISTICATED LADIES

Words and Music by DUKE ELLINGTON,
IRVING MILLS and JUAN TIZOL

62

# DANCING ON THE CEILING

from SIMPLE SIMON
from EVER GREEN

Words by LORENZ HART
Music by RICHARD RODGERS

# DAY BY DAY

## Theme from the Paramount Television Series DAY BY DAY

Words and Music by SAMMY CAHN,
AXEL STORDAHL and PAUL WESTON

# DEARLY BELOVED

from YOU WERE NEVER LOVELIER

Music by JEROME KERN
Words by JOHNNY MERCER

# DO NOTHIN' TILL YOU HEAR FROM ME

Words and Music by DUKE ELLINGTON
and BOB RUSSELL

Moderately Slow

76

# DON'T GET AROUND MUCH ANYMORE

**from SOPHISTICATED LADY**

Words and Music by DUKE ELLINGTON
and BOB RUSSELL

79

# FALLING IN LOVE WITH LOVE

## from THE BOYS FROM SYRACUSE

Words by LORENZ HART
Music by RICHARD RODGERS

86

# A FINE ROMANCE

from SWING TIME

Words by DOROTHY FIELDS
Music by JEROME KERN

# GEORGIA ON MY MIND

Words by STUART GORRELL
Music by HOAGY CARMICHAEL

# GOD BLESS' THE CHILD

Words and Music by ARTHUR HERZOG JR.
and BILLIE HOLIDAY

# HAVE YOU MET MISS JONES?

from I'D RATHER BE RIGHT

Words by LORENZ HART
Music by RICHARD RODGERS

# HELLO, YOUNG LOVERS
## from THE KING AND I

Lyrics by OSCAR HAMMERSTEIN II
Music by RICHARD RODGERS

**Refrain** *(very moderately)*

# HERE'S THAT RAINY DAY
## from CARNIVAL IN FLANDERS

Words by JOHNNY BURKE
Music by JIMMY VAN HEUSEN

# I CAN'T GET STARTED WITH YOU

### from ZIEGFELD FOLLIES

Words by IRA GERSHWIN
Music by VERNON DUKE

# I COULD WRITE A BOOK

## from PAL JOEY

Words by LORENZ HART
Music by RICHARD RODGERS

# I GET ALONG WITHOUT YOU VERY WELL
## (Except Sometimes)

Words and Music by HOAGY CARMICHAEL
Inspired by a poem written by J.B. THOMPSON

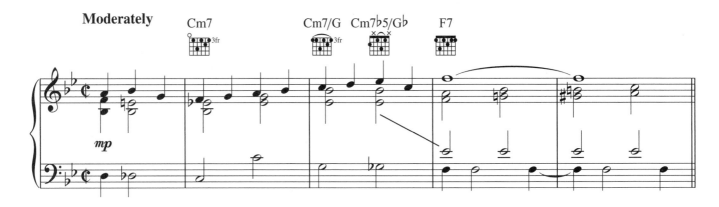

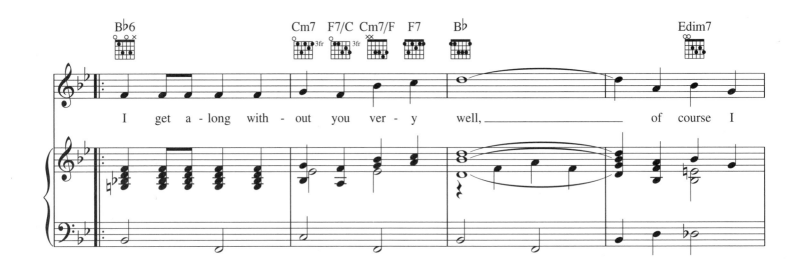

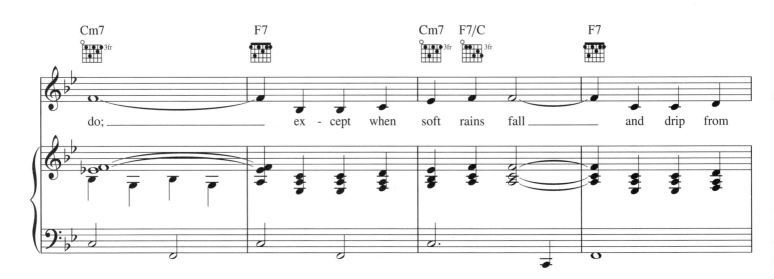

# I GOT IT BAD AND THAT AIN'T GOOD

Words by PAUL FRANCIS WEBSTER
Music by DUKE ELLINGTON

The po-ets say that all who love are blind; but I'm in love and I___ know what time it is! ___ The Good Book says, "Go seek and ye shall find." Well,

133

# I HEAR MUSIC

from the Paramount Picture DANCING ON A DIME

Words by FRANK LOESSER
Music by BURTON LANE

# I'LL NEVER SMILE AGAIN

Words and Music by
RUTH LOWE

# I'LL REMEMBER APRIL

Words and Music by PAT JOHNSTON,
DON RAYE and GENE DE PAUL

# I'M BEGINNING TO SEE THE LIGHT

Words and Music by DON GEORGE, JOHNNY HODGES,
DUKE ELLINGTON and HARRY JAMES

*8vb*

# I'VE GOT YOU UNDER MY SKIN

from BORN TO DANCE

Words and Music by
COLE PORTER

# IMAGINATION

Words by JOHNNY BURKE
Music by JIMMY VAN HEUSEN

157

# IN A SENTIMENTAL MOOD

Words and Music by DUKE ELLINGTON,
IRVING MILLS and MANNY KURTZ

**Slowly, with expression**

In a sen-ti-men-tal mood, _____ I can see the stars come

through my room, _____ while your lov-ing at-ti-tude _____ is like a

flame _____ that lights the gloom. On the wings of ev-'ry

# IN THE WEE SMALL HOURS OF THE MORNING

Words by BOB HILLIARD
Music by DAVID MANN

# ISN'T IT ROMANTIC?

from the Paramount Picture LOVE ME TONIGHT

Words by LORENZ HART
Music by RICHARD RODGERS

# IT MIGHT AS WELL BE SPRING

## from STATE FAIR

Lyrics by OSCAR HAMMERSTEIN II
Music by RICHARD RODGERS

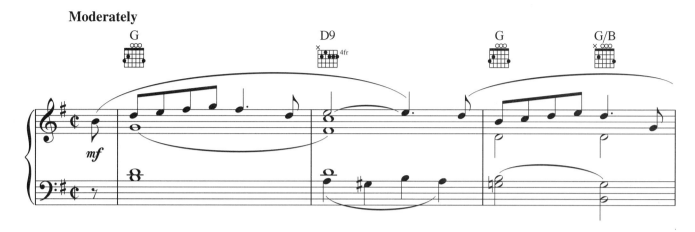

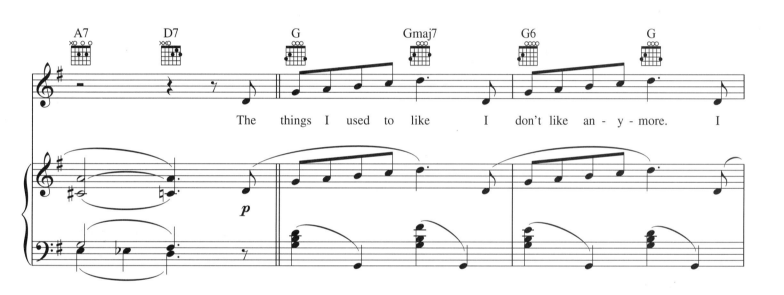

The things I used to like I don't like an-y-more. I

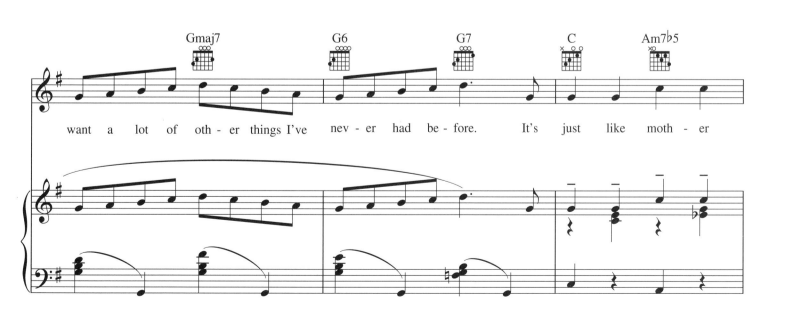

want a lot of oth-er things I've nev-er had be-fore. It's just like moth-er

# IT COULD HAPPEN TO YOU

### from the Paramount Picture AND THE ANGELS SING

Words by JOHNNY BURKE
Music by JAMES VAN HEUSEN

# IT DON'T MEAN A THING
## (If It Ain't Got That Swing)
### from SOPHISTICATED LADIES

Words and Music by DUKE ELLINGTON
and IRVING MILLS

# JUNE IN JANUARY

## from the Paramount Picture HERE IS MY HEART

Words and Music by LEO ROBIN
and RALPH RAINGER

# LOVER

from the Paramount Picture LOVE ME TONIGHT

Words by LORENZ HART
Music by RICHARD RODGERS

# LIKE SOMEONE IN LOVE

Words by JOHNNY BURKE
Music by JIMMY VAN HEUSEN

# LOLLIPOPS AND ROSES

Words and Music by
TONY VELONA

With movement

Tell her you care each time you speak. Make it her birth-day each
One day she'll smile, next day she'll cry, min-ute to min-ute you'll

day of the week. Bring her nice things, su-gar and spice things, ros-es and lol-li-pops and
nev-er know why. Coax her, pet her, bet-ter yet, get her ros-es and lol-li-pops and

lol-li-pops and ros-es. ros-es. We try ___ act-ing grown up, ___ but ___
lol-li-pops and

# LOVER MAN
## (Oh, Where Can You Be?)

By JIMMY DAVIS,
ROGER "RAM" RAMIREZ and JIMMY SHERMAN

I don't wish for rich - es,

I'll not take that chance.

Don't want to be

fa - mous, I on - ly want ro - mance.

# MISTY

Words by JOHNNY BURKE
Music by ERROLL GARNER

202

# MONA LISA

from the Paramount Picture CAPTAIN CAREY, U.S.A.

Words and Music by JAY LIVINGSTON
and RAY EVANS

# MOOD INDIGO

## from SOPHISTICATED LADIES

Words and Music by DUKE ELLINGTON,
IRVING MILLS and ALBANY BIGARD

# MOONLIGHT BECOMES YOU

from the Paramount Picture ROAD TO MOROCCO

Words by JOHNNY BURKE
Music by JAMES VAN HEUSEN

# MY HEART STOOD STILL
## from A CONNECTICUT YANKEE

Words by LORENZ HART
Music by RICHARD RODGERS

# MY OLD FLAME

## from the Paramount Picture BELLE OF THE NINETIES

Words and Music by ARTHUR JOHNSTON
and SAM COSLOW

219

# MY ROMANCE

from JUMBO

Words by LORENZ HART
Music by RICHARD RODGERS

# MY SILENT LOVE

Words by EDWARD HEYMAN
Music by DANA SUESSE

# THE NEARNESS OF YOU

from the Paramount Picture ROMANCE IN THE DARK

Words by NED WASHINGTON
Music by HOAGY CARMICHAEL

# A NIGHT IN TUNISIA

By JOHN "DIZZY" GILLESPIE
and FRANK PAPARELLI

Moderately Fast

241

# OUT OF NOWHERE

**from the Paramount Picture DUDE RANCH**

Words by EDWARD HEYMAN
Music by JOHNNY GREEN

# PICK YOURSELF UP
## from SWING TIME

Words by DOROTHY FIELDS
Music by JEROME KERN

# QUIET NIGHTS OF QUIET STARS
## (Corcovado)

English Words by GENE LEES
Original Words and Music by ANTONIO CARLOS JOBIM

Qui - et nights of qui - et stars,

# SATIN DOLL
## from SOPHISTICATED LADIES

Words by JOHNNY MERCER and BILLY STRAYHORN
Music by DUKE ELLINGTON

# SOPHISTICATED LADY

from SOPHISTICATED LADIES

Words and Music by DUKE ELLINGTON,
IRVING MILLS and MITCHELL PARISH

# STELLA BY STARLIGHT

from the Paramount Picture THE UNINVITED

Words by NED WASHINGTON
Music by VICTOR YOUNG

# SO NICE
## (Summer Samba)

Original Words and Music by MARCOS VALLE
and PAULO SERGIO VALLE
English Words by NORMAN GIMBEL

# A SUNDAY KIND OF LOVE

Words and Music by BARBARA BELLE, LOUIS PRIMA,
ANITA LEONARD and STAN RHODES

Moderately Slow

*mf*

*mp-mf*

**F6**

I want a Sun-day kind of love, __ a love to last past

**Am7**  **Abm7**  **Gm7**  **C7-9**

**Am7**  **D7-9**  **Gm7**  **Bbm6**  **Am7**  **D7**

Sat - ur-day night, __ I'd like to know it's more than love at first sight. __

**Gm7**  **C7+5**  **Bb/C**  **F6**  **Am7**  **Abm7**  **Gm7**  **Abm6**  **E7-5**

I want a Sun-day kind of love. _____ I want a

# THESE FOOLISH THINGS
## (Remind Me of You)

Words by HOLT MARVELL
Music by JACK STRACHEY

**Slowly**

A cig - a-rette that bears a
First daf - fo-dils and long ex -
Gar - de - nia per - fume ling - 'ring

lip - stick's tra - ces,
cit - ed ca - bles,
on a pil - low,

An air - line tick - et to ro - man - tic pla - ces,
And can - dle lights on lit - tle cor - ner ta - bles,
Wild straw - b'ries on - ly sev - en francs a ki - lo,

And still my heart has wings ___ These fool - ish things re - mind me of
And still my heart has wings ___ These fool - ish things re - mind me of
And still my heart has wings ___ These fool - ish things re - mind me of

# TANGERINE

### from the Paramount Picture THE FLEET'S IN

Words by JOHNNY MERCER
Music by VICTOR SCHERTZINGER

# THIS CAN'T BE LOVE

## from THE BOYS FROM SYRACUSE

Words by LORENZ HART
Music by RICHARD RODGERS

# THE VERY THOUGHT OF YOU

Words and Music by
RAY NOBLE

I don't need your pho - to - graph, _____
I hold you re - spon - si - ble, _____

_____ to keep _____ by my bed;
_____ I'll take _____ it to law,

Your pic - ture is
I nev - er have

al - ways in _____ my head. _____
felt like this _____ be - fore. _____

# THOU SWELL

## from A CONNECTICUT YANKEE
## from WORDS AND MUSIC

Words by LORENZ HART
Music by RICHARD RODGERS

# UNFORGETTABLE

Words and Music by
IRVING GORDON

# THE WAY YOU LOOK TONIGHT

## from SWING TIME

Words by DOROTHY FIELDS
Music by JEROME KERN

# YESTERDAYS

from ROBERTA
from LOVELY TO LOOK AT

Words by OTTO HARBACH
Music by JEROME KERN

# WHY DO I LOVE YOU?

## from SHOW BOAT

Lyrics by OSCAR HAMMERSTEIN II
Music by JEROME KERN

# YOU ARE TOO BEAUTIFUL

from HALLELUJAH, I'M A BUM

Words by LORENZ HART
Music by RICHARD RODGERS

# YOU DON'T KNOW WHAT LOVE IS

Words and Music by DON RAYE
and GENE DePAUL

# YOU BROUGHT A NEW KIND OF LOVE TO ME

from the Paramount Picture THE BIG POND

Words and Music by SAMMY FAIN,
IRVING KAHAL and PIERRE NORMAN

Nev-er will I meet one _____ sweet-er than

you. _____ Would you _____

turn a-way or could you _____ real-ly learn to

care If I'd ev-er dare to say, "I love

# THE BEST EVER COLLECTION

## ARRANGED FOR PIANO, VOICE AND GUITAR

**0 of the Most Beautiful Songs Ever**
) ballads: Bewitched • (They Long to Be) Close to You •
How Deep Is Your Love • I'll Be Seeing You •
chained Melody • Yesterday • Young at Heart • more.
360735 .................................................................$24.95

**st Acoustic Rock Songs Ever**
acoustic hits: Dust in the Wind • Fast Car • I Will
member You • Landslide • Leaving on a Jet Plane •
ggie May • Tears in Heaven • Yesterday • more.
310984 .................................................................$19.95

**st Big Band Songs Ever**
er 60 big band hits: Boogie Woogie Bugle Boy • Don't
t Around Much Anymore • In the Mood • Moonglow
Sentimental Journey • Who's Sorry Now • more.
359129 .................................................................$16.95

**st Broadway Songs Ever**
er 70 songs in all! Includes: All I Ask of You • Bess,
u Is My Woman • Climb Ev'ry Mountain • Comedy
night • If I Were a Rich Man • Ol' Man River • more!
309155 .................................................................$22.95

**st Children's Songs Ever**
er 100 songs: Bingo • Eensy Weensy Spider • The
rmer in the Dell • On Top of Spaghetti • Puff the
gic Dragon • Twinkle, Twinkle Little Star • and more.
310360 (Easy Piano) ............................................$19.95

**st Christmas Songs Ever**
re than 60 holiday favorites: Frosty the Snow Man • A
lly Jolly Christmas • I'll Be Home for Christmas •
dolph, The Red-Nosed Reindeer • Silver Bells • more.
359130 .................................................................$19.95

**st Classic Rock Songs Ever**
er 60 hits: American Woman • Bang a Gong • Cold As
• Heartache Tonight • Rock and Roll All Nite •
oke on the Water • Wonderful Tonight • and more.
310800 .................................................................$18.95

**st Classical Songs Ever**
er 80 of classical favorites: Ave Maria • Canon in D •
e Kleine Nachtmusik • Für Elise • Lacrymosa • Ode
Joy • William Tell Overture • and many more.
310674 (Piano Solo) ............................................$19.95

**st Contemporary Christian Songs Ever**
er 70 favorites, including: Awesome God • El Shaddai
Friends • Jesus Freak • People Need the Lord • Place
This World • Serve the Lord • Thy Word • more.
310558 .................................................................$19.95

**st Country Songs Ever**
classic country hits: Always on My Mind • Crazy •
ddy Sang Bass • Forever and Ever, Amen • God Bless
• U.S.A. • I Fall to Pieces • Through the Years • more.
359135 .................................................................$17.95

**st Early Rock 'n' Roll Songs Ever**
er 70 songs, including: Book of Love • Crying • Do
h Diddy Diddy • Louie, Louie • Peggy Sue • Shout •
lish Splash • Stand By Me • Tequila • and more.
310816 .................................................................$17.95

**Best Easy Listening Songs Ever**
75 mellow favorites: (They Long to Be) Close to You •
Every Breath You Take • How Am I Supposed to Live
Without You • Unchained Melody • more.
00359193 ..............................................................$18.95

**Best Gospel Songs Ever**
80 gospel songs: Amazing Grace • Daddy Sang Bass •
How Great Thou Art • I'll Fly Away • Just a Closer Walk
with Thee • The Old Rugged Cross • more.
00310503 ..............................................................$19.95

**Best Hymns Ever**
118 hymns: Abide with Me • Every Time I Feel the Spirit
• He Leadeth Me • I Love to Tell the Story • Were You
There? • When I Survey the Wondrous Cross • and more.
00310774 ..............................................................$17.95

**Best Jazz Standards Ever**
77 jazz hits: April in Paris • Beyond the Sea • Don't Get
Around Much Anymore • Misty • Satin Doll • So Nice
(Summer Samba) • Unforgettable • and more.
00311641 ..............................................................$19.95

**More of the Best Jazz Standards Ever**
74 beloved jazz hits: Ain't Misbehavin' • Blue Skies •
Come Fly with Me • Honeysuckle Rose • The Lady Is a
Tramp • Moon River • My Funny Valentine • and more.
00311023 ..............................................................$19.95

**Best Latin Songs Ever**
67 songs: Besame Mucho (Kiss Me Much) • The Girl from
Ipanema • Malaguena • Slightly Out of Tune
(Desafinado) • Summer Samba (So Nice) • and more.
00310355 ..............................................................$19.95

**Best Love Songs Ever**
65 favorite love songs, including: Endless Love • Here
and Now • Love Takes Time • Misty • My Funny
Valentine • So in Love • You Needed Me • Your Song.
00359198 ..............................................................$19.95

**Best Movie Songs Ever**
74 songs from the movies: Almost Paradise • Chariots of
Fire • My Heart Will Go On • Take My Breath Away •
Unchained Melody • You'll Be in My Heart • more.
00310063 ..............................................................$19.95

**Best Praise & Worship Songs Ever**
80 all-time favorites: Awesome God • Breathe • Here I
Am to Worship • I Could Sing of Your Love Forever •
Open the Eyes of My Heart • Shout to the Lord • more.
00310063 ..............................................................$19.95

**Best R&B Songs Ever**
66 songs, including: Baby Love • Endless Love • Here
and Now • I Will Survive • Saving All My Love for You
• Stand By Me • What's Going On • and more.
00310184 ..............................................................$19.95

**Best Rock Songs Ever**
Over 60 songs: All Shook Up • Blue Suede Shoes • Born
to Be Wild • Every Breath You Take • Free Bird • Hey
Jude • We Got the Beat • Wild Thing • more!
00490424 ..............................................................$18.95

**Best Songs Ever**
Over 70 must-own classics: Edelweiss • Love Me Tender
• Memory • My Funny Valentine • Tears in Heaven •
Unforgettable • A Whole New World • and more.
00359224 ..............................................................$22.95

**More of the Best Songs Ever**
79 more favorites: April in Paris • Candle in the Wind •
Endless Love • Misty • My Blue Heaven • My Heart Will
Go On • Stella by Starlight • Witchcraft • more.
00310437 ..............................................................$19.95

**Best Standards Ever, Vol. 1 (A-L)**
72 beautiful ballads, including: All the Things You Are •
Bewitched • God Bless' the Child • I've Got You Under
My Skin • The Lady Is a Tramp • more.
00359231 ..............................................................$16.95

**More of the Best Standards Ever, Vol. 1 (A-L)**
76 all-time favorites: Ain't Misbehavin' • Always •
Autumn in New York • Desafinado • Fever • Fly Me to
the Moon • Georgia on My Mind • and more.
00310813 ..............................................................$17.95

**Best Standards Ever, Vol. 2 (M-Z)**
72 songs: Makin' Whoopee • Misty • My Funny Valentine
• People Will Say We're in Love • Smoke Gets in Your
Eyes • Strangers in the Night • Tuxedo Junction • more.
00359232 ..............................................................$16.95

**More of the Best Standards Ever, Vol. 2 (M-Z)**
75 more stunning standards: Mona Lisa • Mood Indigo •
Moon River • Norwegian Wood • Route 66 • Sentimental
Journey • Stella by Starlight • What'll I Do? • and more.
00310814 ..............................................................$17.95

**Best Torch Songs Ever**
70 sad and sultry favorites: All by Myself • Crazy • Fever
• I Will Remember You • Misty • Stormy Weather (Keeps
Rainin' All the Time) • Unchained Melody • and more.
00311027 ..............................................................$19.95

**Best TV Songs Ever**
Over 50 fun and catchy theme songs: The Addams Family
• The Brady Bunch • Happy Days • Mission: Impossible
• Where Everybody Knows Your Name • and more!
00311048 ..............................................................$17.95

**Best Wedding Songs Ever**
70 songs of love and commitment: All I Ask of You •
Endless Love • The Lord's Prayer • My Heart Will Go On
• Trumpet Voluntary • Wedding March • and more.
00311096 ..............................................................$17.95

# REAL JAZZ FAKE BOOKS FROM HAL LEONARD

*These magnificent compilations hold over 240 standards of jazz repertoire in each book, containing easy-to-read authentic hand-written jazz engravings. The collections also feature the original harmony, and an alternate harmonization reflecting common practice by many jazz artists, so players can choose to use the traditional version, a hipper version, or a combination of the two! Spiral comb bound.*

## THE HAL LEONARD REAL JAZZ CLASSICS BOOK

Over 300 classic jazz hits, including: After the Rain • Airegin • All Blues • Along Can Betty • Ana Maria • Bags' Groove • Billie's Bounce (Bill's Bounce) • Birdland • Blue in Hoss Flat (Foster/Basie) • Boplicity (Be Bop Lives) • The Champ • Chelsea Bridge A Child Is Born • Don't Be That Way • Emancipation Blues • Epistrophy • Footprints Freddie Freeloader • Giant Steps • Half Nelson • I Waited for You • In Walked Bud Israel • Johnny Come Lately • Jordu • Jump, Jive An' Wail • Lady Bird • Lemon Drop Line for Lyons • Little Waltz • Lullaby of Birdland • Mambo #5 • Miles • Naima (Niema • A Night in Tunisia • One for Daddy • Passion Flower • Peel Me a Grape • Quiet Now Red Top • Robin's Nest • Rosewood • Ruby, My Dear • Seven Come Eleven • Sidewinde • So Far Away • So What • Song for Helen • Stolen Moments • Take Five • Tenor Madnes • Time Remembered • Waltz for Debby • Well You Needn't (It's over Now) • Yardbir Suite • and more.

\_\_\_\_00240162   C Edition ...............................................................................$39.9
\_\_\_\_00240174   B♭ Edition ..............................................................................$39.9
\_\_\_\_00240175   E♭ Edition ..............................................................................$39.9

## THE HAL LEONARD REAL JAZZ STANDARDS FAKE BOOK

246 songs, including: Ain't Misbehavin' • Angel Eyes • Bein' Green • Blue Skies • Braz • Cherokee (Indian Love Song) • Crazy He Calls Me • Darn That Dream • Desafinad (Off Key) • Early Autumn • Easy Living • Fever • For Every Man There's a Woman • Gi Talk • Good Morning Heartache • Here's That Rainy Day • How Little We Know • I Can' Give You Anything but Love • I Didn't Know What Time It Was • I Got It Bad and Tha Ain't Good • I Remember You • I'll Be Around • I'm Beginning to See the Light • I'v Heard That Song Before • Imagination • It Could Happen to You • It's Easy to Rememb • June in January • Lazy Afternoon • Midnight Sun • My Blue Heaven • My One and Onl Love • Mood Indigo • Moonglow • One for My Baby (And One More for the Road) Satin Doll • Sophisticated Lady • Star Dust • Tenderly • When Sunny Gets Blue • an more. Spiral comb bound.

\_\_\_\_00240161   C Edition .................................................................................$39.9
\_\_\_\_00240173   B♭ Edition ..............................................................................$39.9
\_\_\_\_00240172   E♭ Edition ..............................................................................$39.9

FOR MORE INFORMATION, SEE YOUR LOCAL MUSIC DEALER,
OR WRITE TO:

## HAL•LEONARD® CORPORATION

7777 W. BLUEMOUND RD. P.O. BOX 13819 MILWAUKEE, WI 53213

Visit Hal Leonard Online at
**www.halleonard.com**

Prices, contents and availability subject to change without notice.